The glory

 STEIMATZKY'S AGENCY LIMITED

 THE JERUSALEM PUBLISHING HOUSE

# of Masada

Raphael Posner / A. van der Heyden

Design: BOB VARI

Editorial Secretary: Rachel Gilon

© *1981 by G.G. The Jerusalem Publishing House Ltd.,
39 Tchernechovski St., P.O. Box 7147, Jerusalem and
Shlomo S. Gafni, Jerusalem*

Printed in Belgium by Offset Printing Van Den Bossche

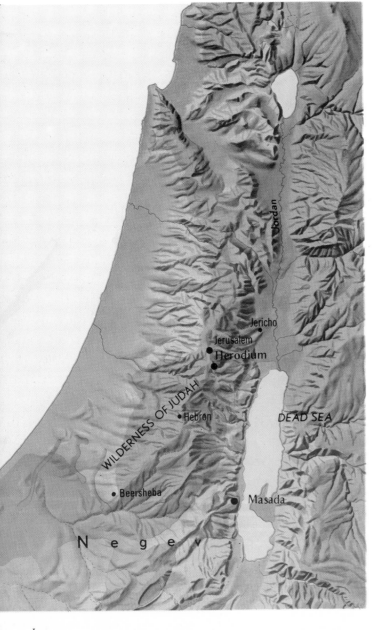

*Endpapers: The view to the west through the columns of
Herod's northern palace.
Title page: Masada from the north-east.
I. Desert flowers. A typical sight on Masada after the rains.
II. The capitals of the columns on the lowest level of the
northern villa rear like crowned heads against the sky.
III. One of the plainer mosaics in Herod's official palace.
IV. The Roman commander's camp seen from the summit.*

I

II

Contents

III

IV

Introduction

Masada is a rock in the desert; it is a luxurious fortress built by a paranoid king; it is 960 patriots fighting for their freedom against the mighty Roman Empire; it is mass suicide when all hope has gone; it is an archaeological expedition of unprecedented scope. Yet, it is more than all that. Masada is a silent monument to extraordinary heroism and a symbol for a reborn nation.

The archaeologists have prepared Masada for the modern explorer. He will find excellent access roads and even a cable car to take him to it in comfort. He will find the ruins reconstructed to a great extent, so he will easily be able to recognize the buildings and their functions. And yet a visit to Masada will bring the explorer face to face with problems more serious than the technicalities of archaeology.

Until the excavations, all that was known of Masada was from Josephus Flavius who, in the 1st century A.D., wrote a history of the Jewish revolt. (He wrote in Greek and our citations are taken from the excellent translation of G.A. Williamson, published by Penguin Books Ltd.) The archaeologists worked with one eye on Josephus, and they discovered that his account was substantially correct. However, the explorer should perhaps try to imagine what the archaeologists' conclusions might have been had Josephus' Jewish War never been written. Would they have been able to reconstruct the dramatic events at Masada, or would they have fitted the thousands of facts they brought to light into a completely different story?

An exploration of Masada is not only a tour through ruins and restored buildings, it is also an investigation of history. In this book we have attempted to give a bird's-eye view of that exciting period in Israel's history. We have not dealt with many of the finer points discussed by historians. For us, the rebels on Masada are Zealots, and we shall not go into the question of which faction of the rebel movement they represented, or what their exact philosophy was. What we have tried to do is to put Masada and its finds into their historical context, and indicate some of the lacunae, and even contradictions, that still exist.

Not surprisingly, the restoration of Masada was undertaken after the establishment of the State of Israel. The fall of Masada has come to represent the end of Jewish freedom in the Holy Land and, as such, it is a very important symbol for Israel. In the one thousand, eight hundred and seventy-four years that elapsed betweeen Masada and Israel's Declaration of Independence in 1948, the country was ruled by successive invaders, starting with the Romans and ending with the British, who invaded the country by virtue of a Mandate granted them by other outside powers. Israelis see themselves as the heirs of the nation whose fall was symbolized by the men, women and children on Masada who refused slavery and chose to die free.

Masada as an archaeological site is extremely impressive; Masada as a story grips the heart and provides an insight into the human soul. It has something important to say to everyone.

Standing on the border of the Judaean Desert and the Dead Sea Valley, it can be seen from kilometres away rearing up out of the desolation that surrounds it. From the west, the visitor must trek over wadis and hills under the blazing sun until he reaches it — 200 metres above him. From the east, he must travel westwards with the Dead Sea at his back, through flat-topped hillocks a few metres high, like miniatures of the mighty mountains in the distance, and there it is, towering 400 metres into the blue sky — Al Saba as the Arabs called it, or Masada as the world knows it today.

1. Masada from the west; the Dead Sea is seen in the background. In the foreground, the assault ramp can be clearly distinguished and, at its foot, the remains of the archaeologists' camp with the modern road from Arad leading to it.

1

For the modern explorer, the approach to Masada is easy; a well-paved road on the east side leads to the foot of the rock where he will find a cable car, very much like those used in Switzerland, ready to take him to the top. Only a few years ago he would have had to get there early in the morning to avoid the heat of the day and make an arduous ascent on foot, 5.5 kilometres, to reach the summit. From the west, too, the approach is relatively comfortable. A modern road cuts through the desert from the new town of Arad and leads to the very foot of the Roman siege ramp. A reasonably easy walk up the side of the mountain brings you to the top. Before the Romans built that ramp in A.D. 72 (or, as many scholars today believe, in 73), you would have been faced with a narrow path rising 200 metres.

2
2. *This view — from the summit looking east — shows the rock formations between Masada and the Dead Sea. The small flat-topped shapes look like smaller versions of the huge mountains that surround the sea.*

3. *Looking to the south-east the sea seems to be within reach of the mountain.*

3

4. *A group of visitors beginning the ascent by way of the assault ramp. This path, on the right of the ramp, offers quite a pleasant climb if the day is not too hot.*

4

5

7

6

5. In this view of Masada from the west the road from Arad can be seen in the left-hand corner. The "steps" at the northern end of the mountain make it easy to identify.

6. The "steps" also stand out in this view from the north-east. The photograph was taken from the road which runs along the west bank of the Dead Sea.

7. Stone markers erected by the men who laid the road along the Dead Sea shore after 1967. The sea and the mountains in the Kingdom of Jordan, on the other bank, provide a setting a sculptor would be delighted with.

The journey to the foot of Masada has its own interests. The Judaean Desert stretches from the eastern side of Jerusalem all the way to the Dead Sea Valley. It is not at all like the fabled Arabian deserts, of endless undulating seas of sand; it is rough, rock-strewn and cut across with wadis. In the winter there one sees little islands of green here and there — a faint memory of the winter rains that pour down but run away to waste. As we come closer to the eastern edge of this wilderness, the canyons become deeper and the hills higher. In the east lies the arid, oppressive Dead Sea Valley. The sea shimmers silvery in the sun, but the atmosphere is heavy with odours of minerals evaporating in this, the lowest spot on earth. Looking westwards from the Dead Sea, the mountains at the edge of the Judaean Wilderness are like a huge wall isolating this somnolent valley from the outside world. An overall view gives an impression that once, long long ago, the entire valley may have been filled with water, and it is easy to believe that you can make out the stages of the water's retreat. But that was a very long time ago, before history.

The massive wall of mountains, however, is not solid. Between the rearing rocks, the wadis of the Judaean Desert find their way to the sea, and in the winter, great torrents of water rush down the wadis to the sea and wash away all that stands in their path — including modern roads. But the Dead Sea remains what it has always been — a salty lake. One recalls Ecclesiastes: "All the rivers run into the sea, yet the sea is never full".

8. One of the wadis west of Masada. The changing shadows emphasize the dramatic outlines of the promontory.

8

9/10. When the winter rains come these wadis are filled with rushing torrents of water sweeping away everything that stands in their path. Boulders are carried along by the water and being trapped in a wadi when it rains is a very dangerous experience. People have actually died of drowning in the desert.

10

9

It was in the first half of the 1st century B.C. that the mighty Roman Empire began to dominate the tiny kingdom of Judaea. In 63 B.C. Pompey, the illustrious Roman general, resolved the dispute over the succession between the two sons of Queen Salome Alexandra and, from that time, Judaea became subservient to Rome, although it still maintained the trappings of independence — a king, a high priest and political institutions. After King Herod died in 4 B.C., there was no longer a king in Judaea, only an "ethnarch". The proud little country which had won its independence by force of arms from the mighty Seleucid kingdom of Syria, was now, in effect, a district of the Roman province of Syria. It might have been assimilated into the Roman Empire, were it not for its religion. Judaism is an exclusive faith which believes in one God and one God only. The Jews could neither respect nor even countenance paganism with its pantheons of gods in different guises and with different names; they could not accept emperor-worship, no matter what sophisticated explanations were given to it. This fanaticism, as the more tolerant peoples saw it, together with the indignity of dependence and the rapacious greed of the Roman procurators, who often bought their posts and expected a good return on their investment, was bound to lead to an explosion.

In the year A.D. 66 the great revolt of the Jews against the Romans started. This revolt, known as the First Roman War or the Great War, was sparked by the rapacious behaviour of the procurator, Florus, in Jerusalem. The Roman garrison in Jerusalem was wiped out, and an expeditionary force sent down from Syria to crush the revolt was defeated on its way to Jerusalem. The Jews set up a provisional government, which even minted coins proclaiming Jewish freedom.

Slowly and inexorably the Roman war machine went into action and the result was really only a matter of time. Jewish communities were annihilated one after the other, and in A.D. 70 the Roman army, under the future emperor, Titus, stood before Jerusalem. The fall of Jerusalem and the destruction of its Temple were a fearful blow to the Jewish people and its messianic hopes. For a while it had seemed as though what had happened in the days of the Maccabees was happening again, but then the dream gave way to bitter reality. Judaea was lost.

11

11. The head of the Roman emperor Augustus, who was officially deified after his death in A.D. 14 and worshipped as a god. These statues were an abomination in the eyes of the Jews.

12

12. An old-timer recites the Psalms at the Western Wall in Jerusalem. The enormous stones are dressed in the Herodian fashion.

At the beginning of the great revolt, Menahem ben Judah the Galilean, one of the leaders of the Zealot faction, had succeeded in capturing Masada from its Roman garrison "by a stratagem", to quote the Jewish commander, Joseph ben Mattityahu, who later became the historian known as Josephus Flavius. This Menahem left a garrison in Masada and returned to Jerusalem aspiring to become the leader of the Jewish people. In the political in-fighting he had several of his opponents assassinated, and went so far as to appear in the Temple attired in royal garb. When he himself was assassinated, his nephew Eleazar ben Yaïr escaped from Jerusalem to Masada and became its commander. In the aftermath of the destruction of Jerusalem and the fall of other Jewish strongholds, fighters and their families fled to Masada, the last remnant of Jewish independence, to hold out and wait for God to deliver His people.

In A.D. 72 (or 73), the Tenth Roman Legion, commanded by Flavius Silva, and accompanied by thousands of Jewish prisoners of war, turned its attention to Masada to put a final end to the revolt.

13. A pillar commemorating the Tenth Roman Legion in the Old City of Jerusalem. No one knows exactly how it got there or where it came from. It is, however, solid evidence of that legion's presence.

13

The story of Masada's role in the war is so powerful that one tends to forget that the mountain did not start its career then. Indeed, it began many many centuries earlier, before recorded history. In 4000 B.C. people lived in caves on the lower part of its southern side. Pieces of broken pottery, mats, cloth and even plants were discovered there, evidence of a Chalcolithic settlement. Fragments of pottery dating from the 10th to the 7th centuries B.C. were found on the summit, but no indications of a permanent settlement there have been discovered. But it does seem that 3,000 years ago some people at least visited the place where the Zealots were to die.

According to Josephus, the fortress was first built, and given the name Masada, by the High Priest Jonathan. The identity of this Jonathan is disputed; some scholars believe that he was the brother of Judas Maccabaeus who lived in the middle of the 2nd century B.C., while others are of the opinion that the reference is to King Alexander Jannaeus, who was also known as Jonathan, and who became both King and High Priest in 103 B.C. Dozens of coins from his reign were discovered on Masada, which is why this identification is more widely accepted. Elsewhere, Josephus attributes the construction of Masada simply to "ancient kings".

14

14. Since time immemorial camels have roamed through the Judaean Desert around Masada. Here a female camel suckles its calf.

15. A sweeping view of one of the wadis west of Masada. When it rains, the water runs down the sides into the course at the bottom, which becomes a powerful stream. The Roman siege wall can be clearly discerned.

15

16

16. *Soft spring greenery clothes the adjoining slopes.*

17

17. 18. *Aerial view of Masada, Herod's giant undertaking:*

1-3. Northern Palace with three terraces; 1. Lower terrace (wall paintings); 2. Middle terrace (columns and pavilion); 3. Upper terrace (balcony and living quarters); 4. Storehouses; 5. Bathhouse; 6. Water Gate; 7. Administration complex; 8. Synagogue; 9. Residential building and Byzantine remnants (where the silver shekel hoard was found); 10. Byzantine chapel; 11. Western Gate; 12. Roman ramp; 13. Silva's camp (Camp F); 14. Herod's Western Palace (with throne room and mosaic); 15. Swimming pool; 16. Columbarium; 17. Southern bastion; 18. Water cistern (underground); 19. Southern Water Gate; 20. Mikvahs; 21. Zealots' apartments; 22. Eastern Gate (Snake Path Gate); 23. Part of Snake Path; 24. Roman camp 1 (partly reconstructed).

The name Masada is also somewhat problematic. In the ancient sources it does not appear in Hebrew, only in Greek transliteration. The accepted view is that it is a form of the Hebrew or Aramaic *matzad*, "fortress".

Following the death of Alexander Jannaeus' widow, Queen Salome Alexandra, the kingdom of Judaea entered a prolonged period of political instability. The Queen's two sons, Aristobulus and Hyrcanus, fought for the throne and the high priesthood, and one of the latter's advisers, Antipater the Idumaean, became an important figure behind the throne. It was this civil war that gave Rome, through Pompey, the opportunity to step into Judaean affairs. Antipater had a gifted son named Herod, who took advantage of the situation to manoeuvre himself into a position of power. To further his ambitions, he married Miriam (in Greek, Mariamne), a princess of the Hasmonaean dynasty, thereby legitimizing his claim to the throne of Judaea, which otherwise, being an Idumaean, he could never have done. In 40 B.C., Mattathias Antigonus, one of the pretenders to the Judaean throne, had himself proclaimed king, with the help of the Parthians, and immediately besieged Herod, his family and entourage in Jerusalem. They managed to escape and made their way to Masada, where Herod left his family and 800 men under the leadership of his brother Joseph, and went to Rome to seek Mark Antony's help to gain the throne. Meanwhile, Antigonus besieged Masada, but was unable to conquer it. Herod, confirmed as King of Judaea, returned at the head of an army and relieved the siege.

After crushing his opposition, Herod became the undisputed ruler of the Holy Land. His reign was bloody and filled with court intrigues, which he usually resolved by executing the parties involved, including his own wife and children. Emperor Augustus is said to have remarked that he would rather be Herod's pig than his son — since Herod was an observant Jew, and did not eat pork, the former had a better chance of surviving!

Between 37 and 31 B.C. Herod, who was the greatest builder the country ever had, transformed Masada into a mighty fortress. According to Josephus, he enclosed the entire plateau with a limestone wall 5.5 metres high and 3.5 metres wide, in which he erected 37 towers, each 23 metres high. The summit itself, which measures more than 600 metres from north to south, and 300 metres from east to west at its widest point, was covered with rich soil, and Herod reserved it for cultivation to ensure that no siege would ever succeed by starving out the defenders. He built several buildings on the summit, including a very luxurious palace at the northern end. Josephus explains Herod's considerations:

"For these preparations indeed, there were very strong reasons; it is believed that Herod equipped this fortress as a refuge for himself, suspecting a double danger — the danger from the Jewish masses, who might push him off his throne and restore to power the royal house that had preceded him, and the greater and more terrible danger from the Egyptian Queen, Cleopatra. For she did not conceal her intentions but constantly appealed to Antony, begging him to destroy Herod, and requesting the transfer to herself of the kingdom of Judaea."

Considering that Antony was infatuated with Cleopatra and gave up everything for her, it is surprising that he did not give her the tiny Jewish kingdom.

Why Masada? — Herod must certainly have had in mind the siege his brother Joseph withstood with only 800 men, but Josephus hints at another good reason. There was plenty of good arable land on the summit of Masada and the fortress could be self-supporting when necessary. With regard to the problem of water, Herod had enormous cisterns cut into the virgin rock, with entry points on the sides of the mountain. Masada's location is such that the flash floods which in winter fill the wadis could be dammed, and aqueducts constructed to lead the water into the cisterns. All the cisterns could be reached from the summit, so that water could be drawn without exposing the besieged.

19

19. The staircase leading into the great cistern at the southern end of the summit.

20. Herod's water system was so good that Masada, though situated in the desert, could afford the luxury of the swimming pool pictured here.

20

21. The opening in the roof of the great cistern. Rain-water was lead to it by a system of conduits and ran into this cistern, where it was stored.

21

22

Did Herod believe that this fortress, however strong and well-provisioned, could have stopped an Egyptian advance had Antony given in to Cleopatra's importunities? The point to remember is that it was not built for that purpose, but rather as a place to which Herod and his family could escape. The nature of the buildings on Masada also indicates, as we shall see, that Herod was more concerned with saving his skin than his country.

Of course, the main consideration for the choice of this particular mountain was its impregnability: on the eastern side the only approach is the tortuous five-and-a-half kilometre climb up the Snake Path, most of which is within sight of the defenders and within the range of their missiles; on the western side the approach was also difficult and dangerous, and Herod made it more so by constructing very strong fortifications there. From the north and the south the summit is virtually unassailable.

Herod himself never had to make use of the refuge in which he had invested so much, and there is no direct evidence that he ever spent time there. After his death it seems that a Roman garrison was stationed there before the Zealots captured it. It is one of the ironies of history that Herod, Rome's faithful servant, had built the fortress in which the final drama of the Jewish revolt against that mighty empire unfolded. But just as the history of Masada did not begin with the Roman War, so, too, it did not end with it. It seems that after the fall of the fortress in A.D. 73 (or 74), a Roman garrison was again stationed there and remained until A.D. 111. In the 5th and 6th centuries some Byzantine monks settled on the summit; this was after a series of earthquakes had destroyed the buildings. The monks built a church decorated with beautiful mosaics which they made in their own workshop. They lived in the ruins and in the many caves scat-

22. A view of Masada at its most desolate. The ground is rocky and uneven and the mountain appears to rear menacingly above it.

23

24

25

tered over the plateau. Crosses were found carved into the walls of some of these caves. It is generally believed that the Christian settlement on Masada ended in the early 7th century, with the Persian and Moslem invasions of the Holy Land. The monks were the last inhabitants of Masada.

The first, and until this century the only, source of information on Masada, Josephus Flavius, was a scion of a prominent priestly family in Jerusalem. When the great revolt began, he was appointed commander of the Galilee, his main task being to fortify that region against the inevitable Roman attack. In the course of the war he was besieged for six weeks in the town of Yotvata (Jotapata), and when it fell he escaped with forty men to a nearby cave. The men resolved to die rather than be taken captive and drew lots to decide who would kill whom. Joseph manipulated the lots so as to be one of the last two. He then persuaded his companion to give up the idea and surrender to the Romans. The Roman commander on the scene was Vespasian, father of the Flavian imperial line, and he seems to have taken to Josephus who became the protégé of the Flavian house, and even called himself Flavius. It was at this stage in his life that he wrote his two great works, *The Jewish War* and *The Antiquities of the Jews*. Though Josephus has been denigrated for his cowardice, there is no doubt that his books — biased though they be — are among the main sources on ancient Jewish history, particularly of his own fateful age.

In 1838, Edward Robinson, an American orientalist who is especially known for his discoveries in Jerusalem, correctly identified Masada. He did not actually get up there, but viewed it through a telescope from Ein Gedi. The first modern visitor to Masada was the American missionary S.W. Wolcott, in 1842. He was followed, six years later, by the members of an

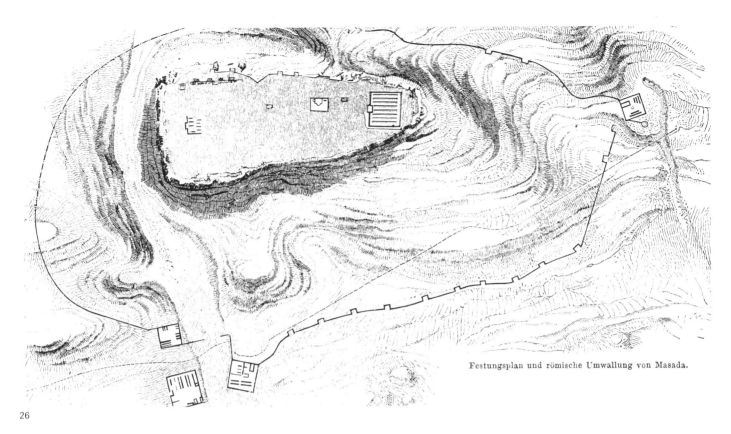

Festungsplan und römische Umwallung von Masada.

26

American naval expedition which was exploring the Jordan Valley and the
Dead Sea. In 1851 the French archaeologist Caignar de Saulcy made the
first survey of the site and drew a plan of the summit. It seems that he had
his Bedouin guides excavate the ruins of the Byzantine church and took
some pieces of the mosaic floor with him as mementos; these pieces ended
up in The Louvre. Modern archaeologists blame de Saulcy for the ruin of
that beautiful mosaic.

In 1867, Sir Charles Warren, a British Army officer and archaeologist,
headed the official Survey of Western Palestine, and, together with Claude
Condor, another officer on the Survey, climbed the Snake Path to the summit, of which he made a very accurate map. At the beginning of the 20th
century, further examinations of the site were made, and attention was
also drawn to the Roman camps around the base of the mountain. Understandably, the exploration of Masada was given great impetus after the establishment of the State of Israel. The twisting Snake Path was traced by S.
Guttman, and Azaryah Alon conducted a detailed examination of the Herodian water system. The years 1955 and 1956 saw large-scale surveys of
Masada, and in 1963 Yigael Yadin, formerly chief of staff of the Israel
Defence Forces and by then professor of archaeology at the Hebrew Uni-
versity, headed the expedition. The dig lasted eleven months, spread over
two seasons, and culminated in the restoration of Masada. Yadin's expedition was supported by several public bodies, including a leading British
newspaper, and enlisted thousands of volunteers from all over the world.
The Israel Defence Forces provided logistic support, and the work became
something of a national effort. Without doubt, the excavation of Masada
was one of the largest archaeological expeditions ever to have been mounted.

*23/24. Caves on the summit. Many of
these were used for dwellings; they were
also occupied by the Byzantine monks
who were the last inhabitants of Masada.
25. A page from a 15th-century manuscript
of Josephus' "Antiquities of the Jews".
Josephus is the only contemporary source
for the drama of Masada, and the
discoveries of the modern excavations all
seem to fit his descriptions.
26. Masada as depicted by the draughts-
men of "Jerusalem und Das Heilige
Land" by Dr. Nepomuk J. Sepp (1873).
The map is amazingly accurate in its
general features though lacking in detail.*

Even before Flavius Silva filled in the wadi to the west and built his assault ramp, Masada could be approached by one of two paths — from the west and from the east. The western path was easier, and Herod had massive fortifications constructed at the point where it reached the summit; two "Columbarium" towers dominate that area.

The course of the western path is no longer visible because the Romans built their enormous assault ramp on the western side of the mountain and thus obliterated it, except for the section from the top of the ramp to the summit. The assault ramp itself is significant because it is a direct illustration of the Roman siege techniques and one of the only examples

27. Silva's assault ramp completely filled the wadi and covered the original western path. This picture conveys a good impression of the manpower that must have been required to construct this enormous ramp.

27

28. Visitors on the path which runs along the side of the assault ramp. Except for the cable car on the east, this is by far the easiest approach.

28

in the world. This was the sort of operation that only a large army could execute because of the complicated logistics involved.

Most of Masada's early explorers made their ascent from the west, climbing up the assault ramp and then up a primitive path to the summit. The Byzantine monks also used the western approach, as is clear from the stone gateway they built at its head. Henry Baker Tristam, the noted naturalist, visited Masada in 1864 and in 1871. He felt that the earlier explorers had exaggerated the difficulty of the western approach on the ramp and remarks that an "English lady" could make the climb without difficulty.

Professor Yadin set up his camp on the western side and the ramp approach was used by his team. The path from the end of the ramp to the summit was improved and a cable-lift was installed to get the heavy equipment to the top.

The eastern path was extremely difficult and, as we shall see, there was no need to protect its point of entry into the plateau. This is the famous Snake (or Serpentine) Path, so called because it twists and turns and zigzags its way up the side of the mountain, rising 400 metres in the course of its 5.5 kilometres. Josephus describes it thus:

"They call the first one [path] the Snake, with reference to its narrowness and constant windings: it is broken as it rounds the projecting cliffs and often turns back on itself, then, lengthening out again a little at a time, manages to make some trifling advance. Walking along it is like balancing on a tightrope. The least slip means death, for on either side yawns an abyss so terrifying that it could make the boldest tremble."

(In fact, either Josephus never made the climb himself, and wrote his description on the basis of tales told by others, or he was not a good climber; the climb is not easy, but it is by no means as terrifying as he makes it out to be.)

29

29. *At the eastern foot of Masada.*
30. *The Snake Path as it appears in "Jerusalem und Das Heilige Land" by Dr. Nepomuk J. Sepp (1873).*
The drawing is wrong, since the "steps" of the northern palace are to the right of the path, not to the left, as they appear here.
31. *Part of the Snake Path, as seen from the ascending cable car.*

30

31

In the course of the centuries the path became covered in some places and obliterated in others; now, however, it has been restored, and the energetic explorer can climb up it. Before the reconstruction of Masada, it was virtually the only approach, as it was difficult to reach the western foot of the mountain. In those days, climbing the Snake Path was a favourite project of youth movement groups, and the last part was negotiated by means of ropes and other mountaineering devices. After Masada was restored, a cable car was installed to take the more sedentary explorers to the top, but not without a good deal of public dispute. Some people objected on grounds of nature preservation; others held that the cable car made it altogether too easy, and that Masada should be reached after the physical exertion which creates the right frame of mind.

32

32. The Snake Path begins its ascent of the mountain.

33. One of the cable cars photographed from another. The Roman siege camp can be clearly seen near the parked cars and service buildings at the foot.

33

The plateau on the summit is surrounded by a wall, and at the point where the Snake Path reaches it there is an entrance known as the Snake Path Gate. This suggests that the path was a commonly-used route in ancient times.

The surrounding wall is a casemate one, i.e., it consists of two walls roofed over, with partitions dividing the inner space into chambers. It is like a long narrow building encircling the plateau. This structure served several objectives — defence, living accommodation and storage areas. The wall is approximately 1,400 metres long and 4 metres wide (exclusive of the thickness of the two walls themselves), and it enclosed most of the plateau. In addition to the rooms, or cells, in the wall, some 30 towers (according to Josephus, 37) rose along its length. The historian states that the wall was 6 metres high and the towers 25 metres high. This sounds exaggerated, but it is no longer possible to check these figures, as over the centuries the entire wall collapsed, due to earthquakes, and it is nowhere complete with the roof. Josephus also reports that the wall was made of limestone; it is actually constructed of rock quarried on the summit or on the upper slopes. On the northern part of the summit, just below the storehouses, there is a huge underground quarry from which, presumably, the stones were taken. However, the wall was plastered, and that may have given the impression of limestone.

34

35

34. The Snake Path Gate.
35. Inside a Zealot dwelling in the casemate wall near the Snake Path Gate.

36

36. A general view of the casemate wall on the western side of the plateau.

The excavators counted more than 100 rooms of various sizes in the wall. The rooms served the Zealots, who divided some of them with partitions to give the families a modicum of privacy. They also installed household equipment in the rooms, notably cooking stoves. The floor in these chambers was the bare, uneven rock of the plateau, and there does not seem to have been any attempt to level it. The living space afforded by the wall was not sufficient for the 960 persons in Masada, and so here and there they added small dwellings against the wall or against other buildings on the summit. These houses were of poor quality and constructed of much smaller stones than the earlier buildings. The Zealots had neither the great resources, nor the interest in comfort and beauty of the royal builder of the fortress.

37. *The living quarters in the wall were equipped with all the necessities for a "normal" life, such as this domestic installation which was used for baking a type of bread.*

37

38. *Dwellings at the south-eastern wall. It is usually easy to spot the Zealot additions, which were built of smaller stones than the original wall.*

38

To the archaeologist the rooms in the casemate wall were a treasure trove. In them was found a great number of day-to-day utensils of the Zealot population. These items provide first-hand information about life in that age and place. Thanks to the thin dry atmosphere on these desert heights, most of the finds, though broken, were in good condition, and pots even retained the soot of the cooking stoves. As Professor Yadin describes the discovery: "...We had the feeling that it had only just been abandoned; for there was a familiar domestic atmosphere...". Along with household utensils, various objects of cosmetic use were discovered, as well as buttons, keys, belt-buckles and rings. In fact, all the accessories of everyday life. Most of the utensils were of pottery, but some were made of bronze, stone and even seashells. The stone vessels are very

39. Cosmetic utensils discovered in rooms in the casemate wall. The Zealots lived on Masada for a considerable period and led normal lives, including "beauty treatment" for the women.

39

40. These well-made domestic utensils found in Masada indicate the high level of craftsmanship in that period. The archaeologists found quite a few such objects.

40

significant. The Zealots were extremely religious Jews who kept the laws of ritual purity meticulously. According to these, stone vessels do not become ritually impure. Other important finds include well-preserved pieces of cloth. These are the oldest specimens found of cloth from the Roman period, and they are still extremely beautiful — well-woven and gracefully coloured.

As well as fighting men, the Zealot community on the mountain included women and children, and they lived there for a considerable time. During their stay a pattern of social life must have developed and, certainly, family life with all its trivia continued. The wives cooked and laundered and beautified themselves; the children played and squabbled, and were taught. The evidence of these mundane activities was found mainly in the rooms of the casemate wall. One of the rooms of the wall, to the south of the Snake Path Gate, served as a bakery.

41. This hole in one of the dwellings in the eastern wall presents a magnificent view of the Dead Sea with the haze-covered mountains of Moab in the background.

41

42

42. Some of the equipment in the bakery in the western section of the casemate wall.

More than 700 ostraca (pieces of pottery with writing on them) were discovered in Masada. For ordinary, everyday use the ostraca served the purpose of today's writing paper, papyrus being too expensive. Many of the shards have only names written on them, mostly Hebrew ones, while others are marked with ciphers and may have served as ration coupons. The writing was all executed by trained scribes. One piece of a wine jar bore the legend "To Herod, King of Judaea". The wine came from Italy which would seem to indicate that the king did at least visit his fortress.

Evidence of the Zealots' preparations to defend the mountain was also discovered in these wall chambers. Enormous rolling-stones, each weighing as much as 50 kilogrammes, were found lying on the floor in some of the rooms. These had probably been kept on the roof, to be rolled down on the attackers, but they were not used because the Romans concentrated their assault at one point on the western side. When the wall collapsed the stones fell into the rooms.

43

43. These ballista-stones were discovered in the Room of the Scrolls in the casemate wall. They apparently fell in from the roof when the wall collapsed.

There were many important finds on Masada, but among the most significant were the scroll fragments. In all archaeological exploration in the Holy Land the great hope is to find the written word which constitutes explicit history. This is particularly true with regards to biblical texts, and especially when it is possible to date the finds precisely. Over the centuries the Hebrew text of the Bible became fixed, and it is the ambition of all biblical scholars to discover ancient scrolls which will either agree or disagree with the version we know.

In a room in the wall on the west were found fragments of the Book of Psalms. They were in such good condition that the archaeologists were at once able to identify them; after the fragments had been treated and photographed on infra-red film the text was quite legible and proved to be chapters 81 to 85. At the same spot the diggers also found a hoard of silver shekels marked Year 1, Year 2, Year 3, Year 4 and Year 5. The numbers indicate the year (of the revolt against Rome) in which the coin was minted, and this suggests the scroll fragments were probably no later than Year 5, i.e., A.D. 70. The text of the fragments and the division into chapters is much the same as the traditional Jewish version. This was true of all the biblical scrolls discovered.

44. Fragment of the Ben Sira Scroll, one of the scrolls discovered on Masada which have made a great contribution to our understanding of that tumultuous period of history.

45. Remains at Qumran on the Dead Sea to the north of Masada. The discovery of one of the Dead Sea Scrolls at Masada suggests that members of the Qumran sect participated in the great Jewish revolt.

44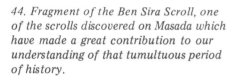

45

In addition to the biblical texts, fragments of other books were also found in some of the rooms. The most important was part of the book of Ecclesiasticus, or the Wisdom of Ben Sira, which was discovered in a chamber near the Snake Path Gate. Ecclesiasticus is an apocryphal work which was not included in the canon of the Jewish Bible; written about the 2nd century B.C., it was exceedingly popular in its time. However, the original Hebrew text was lost since the Middle Ages, and the work was known primarily from a Greek translation done by the author's grandson. In 1896 Solomon Schechter discovered fragments of a Hebrew version of Ben Sira in the Cairo Geniza. (The Geniza was the attic of an ancient Cairo synagogue in which unused and damaged holy books were stored. Thousands of manuscripts were discovered there and scholars are still sorting and identifying them today.) Over the years several other Hebrew versions of Ben Sira were discovered and scholarly battles have been waged between the adherents of this or that version as being the original Hebrew. The Masada find of Chapters 39 to 44 has had a decisive effect in establishing which was the original Hebrew text.

Another interesting literary find was a scroll identical with one of the Dead Sea Scrolls. The latter were written by the scribes of a Jewish sect that lived at Qumran, near the Dead Sea. This was a separatist and ascetic group that rejected the religious establishment in Jerusalem and retired to that desolate region to live in semi-monastic seclusion. Josephus and other sources identify these sectarians with the Essenes; other scholars believe that they were, in fact, Zealots. The discovery of one of their scrolls in Masada raises interesting questions. The latter school of historians holds that the find verifies their theory. For if the Qumran people were Essenes, what was a sectarian scroll doing in a stronghold of orthodoxy?

46. The Qumran Caves in which the scrolls were found by a wandering Bedouin lad. The discovery of the scrolls was one of the sensations of the century, throwing light on the spiritual and social conditions from which early Christianity emerged.

46

Professor Yadin believes that the Qumran people were, indeed, Essenes; however, he is of the opinion that although they disagreed with the religious leadership they were nevertheless Jewish patriots, and took part in the revolt against Rome. If he is correct, the stand at Masada was an all-Jewish one, embracing sectarian groups. Of course, were it not for Josephus, the discovery of that scroll in Masada would probably have led the scholars to identify it as a stronghold of the Qumran sect!

Silver and copper coins were found all over the place, particularly in the wall chambers. In many cases they were discovered scattered on the floors as though their owners knew that they would have no further use for them. Many of the coins were in mint condition, while others were worn.

Following the casemate wall southwards from the Snake Path Gate, we reach the Southern Gate. This one is located near the southernmost point of the wall, and it led to an enormous cistern on the slope. It is entered from the summit by a long staircase. It appears that the cistern was fed by flash floods and rain-water, as were the northern ones (see below). There are several caves near the cisterns, which may have been part of the water system. In one of these caves, however, the archaeologists made a dramatic discovery — the skeletons of some 25 people.

47. This stairway, hewn out of the virgin rock, leads into the enormous storage cistern at the southern end of the plateau. It was used by the inhabitants to get down into the cistern to fetch water.

47

48

Josephus' account of the mass suicide just before the fall of Masada raised an important question in the minds of the archaeologists: where were the bodies of the 960 defenders? We know that after the fall of Masada a Roman garrison was stationed there, and it is unlikely that the bodies would have been left on the summit. What did they do with them? A pathological examination of the bones discovered in the cave below the Southern Gate showed that some were men (up to the age of 70), women (up to the age of 22) and children (under 12). There was also a skeleton of an unborn foetus. It is unlikely that these were remains of Roman soldiers, and a detailed examination of the skulls showed characteristics resembling the ones found in the Bar Kokhba Caves — which were certainly Jewish. The cave may, of course, have served as a burial place for defenders who died in the course of the siege, but the bones were found in great disorder and do not seem to have been interred. Another possibility is that these were the remains of bodies which the Romans found when they entered Masada, and that they threw them into the cave. Perhaps they tossed the rest of the bodies over the side of the mountain.

48. The interior of the great southern cistern. You can gauge its size in relation to the man sitting on the steps. The cistern was hewn out of the rock, and the walls plastered over to reduce the seepage of the water into the stone. This must have been a considerable feat of engineering.

49

Of the four gates in the surrounding wall, two — the Snake Path and the Western — were used for entering and leaving the fortress. The other two were "water gates", i.e., access openings for water carriers. As indicated above, the water supply was one of the main problems of Masada, and Herod's planners devoted much ingenuity to creating a supply and storage system not only for drinking, but also for such luxuries as bathhouses and swimming pools. On the north-western slopes of Masada, just below the summit, Herod had 12 enormous cisterns carved out of the rock and plastered with lime, so that the water would not filter through the porous rock. The water was led into these cisterns by aqueducts from the dams that collected rain- and flash-flood water. Unfortunately the aqueducts were destroyed in the construction of the great ramp. There were other cisterns on the summit, which were filled with rain-water, or with water carried from the flood cisterns. Josephus describes the system:

49. One of the original plastered conduits near the Snake Path Gate. By this method rain-water, running down the sides of the mountain, was collected and led into the storage cisterns.

50. The western side of Masada at the northern extremity. In this area Herod had 12 enormous storage cisterns excavated in the rock, and a complicated system of channels and dams to lead the flood waters into them. Unfortunately, this system has been largely destroyed.

50

"At every spot where people lived, whether on the plateau, round the palace, or before the wall, he [Herod] had cut out in the rock numbers of great tanks to hold water, ensuring a supply as great as where spring water can be used."

The 12 northern cisterns alone have a capacity of 40,000 cubic metres, which is a considerable amount of water. This was in addition to the other cisterns on the summit and on the southern slopes of the mountain.

Flavius Silva, the Roman commander, was faced with very serious problems when he approached Masada. His own logistics were by no means easy: he was in the middle of a wilderness far from food and water supplies, and he had an army to feed. He probably solved this by employing the thousands of Jewish captives Josephus says he brought with him. Silva knew that he could not starve the defenders into submission. He had no alternative but to assault the stronghold. This was the last pocket of Jewish

51

51. Another of the water storage pools. In this one the roof has caved in but remains of the plastered walls can still be seen. There are several such pools on Masada; the inhabitants were never short of water.

52

52. This corner of the great cistern at the southern end of the summit gives some idea of the extent of the plastering that was done in the water storage pools. Every drop of water was precious and the effort invested to prevent seepage was worthwhile.

resistance to Rome and it was held by desperate fanatics. It was also important that none of them escape to spark off other revolts in the rest of the country. Silva, therefore, built a siege wall around the entire mountain; this is known technically as circumvallation. The length of the wall was almost four kilometres and watch towers were spaced along it. To house the troops, the Romans constructed eight camps around the base of Masada. Some of the camps were outside the siege wall while others were part of

53. *The Roman siege camp to the southeast of Masada, near the cable car terminal. This camp has been partly reconstructed.*

53

54. *This siege camp, also at the eastern foot of Masada, was built a short distance from the siege-wall.*

54

it. The camps, two of which were quite large, were constructed in the symmetrical Roman fashion and their vestiges — as well as those of the siege wall — can be clearly seen from the summit today. During the 19th century, some exploration was carried out on the site of the camps, and one has been partly reconstructed, but they represent the last real challenge for Masada archaeologists who, we can assume, will find a wealth of artefacts there from the Roman period.

55. This Roman camp was built up against the siege-wall. The rubble seen in the camps is from the walls which collapsed in the course of the centuries.

55

56. Flavius Silva's camp opposite the assault ramp. From here staff officers could observe the progress of the siege.

56

Silva set up his command headquarters in the camp (known as Camp F) north-west of the mountain. Josephus explains the choice:

"He [Flavius Silva] *established his own headquarters at a place that seemed most opportune for directing the siege, where the rocks on which the fortress stood were linked to the mountains near by, though it was an awkward position for bringing up necessary supplies. For not only was food brought from a distance, at the cost of painful toil for the Jews detailed for the task; even drinking-water had to be fetched to the camp, as the neighbourhood possessed no spring. The preliminary dispositions completed, Silva began the siege operations, which called for great skill and immense exertions in view of the strength of the fortress . . ."*

57. A view from the summit of the Roman camps and the circumvallation to the west. This is a good illustration of the difficult terrain.

West of Masada rises a promontory which Josephus calls the *Leuce*, or White Cliff, and it was from here that Flavius Silva started his assault. First the wadi had to be filled in, and this was no doubt also done by the Jewish captives. An enormous ramp was built across the wadi, rising to a point on the side of the mountain about 50 metres below the summit. On top of this they built what Josephus calls "a pier composed of great stones", to a height of approximately 25 metres. The ramp remains, and is still the western approach to the summit; but the great stones of the pier have long since disappeared. Siege engines, of the type invented by Vespasian and used by his son Titus in the siege of Jerusalem, were then brought up the platform, and an armoured 30-metre tower was erected to protect the teams working the engines. From this tower the Romans shot arrows at the defenders as well as stones somewhat larger than tennis balls from quick-loading catapults. This kept the defenders away from the side under attack and, indeed, hundreds of the stone missiles were discovered at this spot during the excavation. Josephus continues:

"Silva had a great Ram constructed; now by his orders it was swung continuously against the wall till at long last a breach was made and a small section of the wall collapsed."

This breach was the beginning of the end, but the defenders made one last effort. At the place of the breach they constructed an earthwork wall within a wooden framework. As the ram battered this structure, it only pounded the earth into a more solid state, since the wooden planks holding it together were flexible.

"To the enemy the rampart looked like a normal construction, but the blows of the engines falling on a yielding earth were absorbed: the concussion shook it together and made it more solid. Seeing this, Silva decided

58/59. Roman siege equipment constructed in situ for a film about Masada. The producers were advised by historians and archaeologists.

58

59

that fire was the best weapon against such a wall and instructed his men to direct a volley of burning torches at it. Being made mostly of wood it soon caught fire: owing to its loose construction the whole thickness was soon ablaze and a mass of flames shot up."

To any rational person it must have been clear from the outset that ultimately Masada would fall. It might go quickly or it might take longer, but Masada with its 960 defenders — many of them women and children — could not defy the might of Rome indefinitely. The defenders, however, were not thinking rationally. They were waiting for a miracle and, after the earthwork wall caught fire, it suddenly seemed that the miracle was taking place.

"Just as the fire broke out a gust of wind from the north alarmed the Romans: it blew back the flame from above and drove it in their faces, and as their engines seemed on the point of being consumed in the blaze they were plunged into despair."

But it did not last.

"Then, all of a sudden, as if by divine providence, the wind swung to the south, and blowing strongly in the reverse direction carried and flung the flames against the wall, turning it into one blazing mass. God was indeed on the side of the Romans, who returned to camp full of delight, intending to assail the enemy early next day . . ."

Josephus Flavius, the Roman court historian, was in a delicate position. He was writing for the Romans, in whose empire he believed. But a Jewish reader needs to be charitable, indeed, to forgive the former Joseph ben Mattityahu for stating so baldly that God, too, was on the side of the Romans . . .

60. The Romans swarmed onto the summit by way of the assault ramp to the west, only to find desolation and death.

Herod had designed Masada as a royal fortress and Herod was very much a king. He seems to have had a premonition that he would not leave a dynasty which would commemorate his name, so he became one of the greatest builders of his age. His major achievement was the reconstruction of the Temple in Jerusalem, that had been built, on a much more modest scale, after the return of the Babylonian exiles. The sages of the Talmud said, "He who has not seen the Temple has never seen beauty in his life!", and the Roman historian Dio Cassio described the Temple and the palace complex around it as one of the wonders of the world. Herod built several cities — of which the best known is Caesarea — and fortresses, notably Herodion, not far from Bethlehem in the Judaean Desert. He built on a grand royal scale, in Roman style, and Masada was no exception.

61. The Temple which Herod renewed and extended in Jerusalem. This is part of a scale-model of the Holy City in Second Temple times, at the Holyland Hotel in modern Jerusalem.

61

On the western side of the summit, south of where the Romans breached the wall, stands what is known as the Western Palace. This was the King's official residence, with a throne room and administrative offices. This was the largest structure on the plateau — dozens of rooms spread over approximately 4,000 square metres — and was intended for formal occasions, such as royal receptions, as well as for the administration of the "kingdom of Masada". The palace had four wings. The first, built around a courtyard, housed the royal apartments, a large reception hall and the throne room. The reception hall was paved with a magnificent mosaic, parts of which are still extant; in the throne room there are four cavities in the floor in which the legs of the throne were fixed. The royal wing also contained bathrooms and a cold-water pool. Most of the floors were paved with mosaic.

62. One of the reception rooms in the great Western Palace. This area leads into what was presumably the throne room.

62

63. The mosaic floor of the bathroom in the Western Palace. The additions were made during the Zealot occupation.

63

The archaeologists found this area of the palace covered with enormous quantities of ash and rubble, in which hundreds of pieces of broken bronze vessels were discovered. These utensils had no doubt been used in the palace. The courtyard walls had been plastered, in the Herodian fashion, to give the illusion of marble, and the remains of two plastered stone columns were also discovered. The amount of rubble led the archaeologists to the conclusion that the palace had had two storeys. The mosaic in the reception hall had been broken up by treasure hunters, apparently after the fall of the Zealots, but fortunately only one section was vandalized and the eastern portion was left intact. It consists of geometrical figures with as many as six radiating borders in stylized floral motifs. It is believed to be the earliest mosaic of its kind found in the country, and is certainly the most beautiful. Another mosaic floor was found in the passage leading to the bathroom, and it is almost complete. Though not as magnificent as the one in the reception hall, it is nevertheless a fine example of the art.

The royal bathroom is another example of the luxuriousness of the palace. It contains a bathtub with running water, and a cold-water pool. In one of the walls there is a recess for an oil lamp. The bathroom floor was also paved with mosaics, albeit in a simpler design.

In addition to the royal apartments, the Western Palace also contained servants' quarters, kitchens, workshops, administrative offices and large storerooms. In the northern section the excavators discovered an underground cistern which was fed by rain-water from the roof. In fact, the palace was an independent, self-sufficient entity. Several small buildings were discovered near the Western Palace. They were all richly decorated and fitted out and were probably individual residences for members of the

64

64. A winged visitor at the Western Palace. No doubt its ancestors also visited here.

65

65. Although this mosaic in the Western Palace is plainer than many of the others, its precision is quite amazing.

royal family. Between these and the Western Palace there is a large swimming pool, with plastered steps leading down one side. In the walls around the pool one can still see the niches intended for the bathers' clothes. It is all quite remarkably modern. From the coins and other articles found on the bottom of the pool, it is clear that this royal facility was also used by the more spartan Zealots.

66. *The plastered steps leading down into the swimming pool.*

66

67. *Niches in the wall for the bathers' clothing and belongings.*

67

68.

68. *A general view of the storehouses, both those which were reconstructed and those which were left as they were found.*

Masada was intended to house a large garrison in addition to the royal entourage and, obviously, arrangements had to be made to feed the occupants, particularly in times of siege. Joining the two northern extremities of the wall was found a block of storehouses which could only be entered through one gate. Several of the storehouses have been reconstructed and they are as impressive today as they were to Josephus:

"The provisions stored inside were even more astonishing in their abundance and diversity, and in their perfect preservation. The stores included a great quantity of corn — more than enough to last for many years — and quantities of wine and oil, with pulse of all varieties and dates in great heaps."

Herod, it seems, anticipated the necessity of a long stay in his desert fortress, and provided for any emergency.

The excavation of the storehouses was an exceedingly difficult task. The walls and roofs had collapsed in the course of the centuries. Since the Masada dig was undertaken not only in order to enrich archaeological knowledge of the period, but also to restore the site, it was decided to rebuild first and then excavate. The archaeologists could thus utilize the vast quantities of stone that had to be removed anyway. Several of the storehouses were restored and others were left as they had been found. The visitor can thus get a clear impression of the extent of the work. In the storehouses, as in all the other buildings, the archaeologists indicated the extent of the reconstruction by a thick black painted line: the area of wall under the line is the part that was discovered standing, that above the line is the reconstruction.

69. *The black line indicates the extent of the reconstruction. The sections above the line were built by Yigael Yadin's expedition from stones found on the spot.*

69

70

71

70. *The storehouse with the pits in the floor.*

71. *This photograph illustrates the work required to clear the rubble and restore the storehouses.*

The storehouses are long and narrow, much like modern ones. Apparently, each storehouse was used for a specific commodity, and there was at least one for the storage of liquids, such as oil and wine. Here there were three small pits sunk into the floor, to collect liquid spilled while being poured from the large containers into smaller ones. They also facilitated the thorough cleaning of the floor. A great number of artefacts were discovered in the storehouses, including earthenware vessels and coins. Many of the vessels were marked, some with the owners' names and others with ritual markings indicating that the contents were tithes reserved for priestly use.

All except two of the excavated and restored storehouses had been burned, the exceptions being completely empty. Now Josephus reported that the Zealots had decided not to destroy their food supplies, so as to show the Romans that they had not killed themselves in despair because

72. *A building near the storehouses. Apparently this was part of the administration complex.*

72

their supplies had run out. Why then were the storehouses burned? Did the Romans set fire to the buildings? — It seems unlikely that a Roman garrison would destroy perfectly good food. Professor Yadin suggests that the Zealots left two well-stocked chambers to prove their point, and set fire to the rest. The Roman troops made use of the provisions they found, which is why the intact storehouses were found empty.

The regulation of life on Masada required a certain amount of administration, particularly for the distribution of food. This would have been true whether the occupants were King Herod and his entourage, or the Zealot community. Notwithstanding the excellent food supplies, Masada was a fortress, and a system of rationing was necessary, though it may have been quite liberal. The administration of the fortress was housed in a large building adjoining the storehouses to the west. In fact, entrance to the latter was through a gatehouse, also uncovered, that was part of the administration building. Since the Zealots had to deal with the problems that

73

73. One of the buildings near the large bathhouse. The ornamental columns suggest that this building had some official function.

74

74. This bench was part of the entrance into the storehouse complex. The plastering was meant to create the impression of marble.

Herod had prepared for, it is reasonable to suppose that they used this facility for its original purpose. They did, however, make one addition — a *mikvah*, a ritual bath.

75. *The* mikvah *(ritual bath) in the northern administration complex.*

75

76. *The* mikvah *in the south-eastern section of the casemate wall. This picture, as well as the preceding one, clearly shows the intricate planning invested in the construction of a* mikvah. *The different pools are clearly evident.*

76

Many of the discoveries on Masada show that the Zealots were not only fanatical nationalists, but also extremely pious, observant Jews. For them, as for orthodox Jews to this day, a ritual bath is an essential facility. If, as has been suggested, Essenes or members of the Qumran group were among the defenders, the need for it would have been even greater, because these people purified themselves constantly. The *mikvah* is a specially-designed bath and full immersion in it is required to remove any ritual impurity. Women are required to immerse themselves in a *mikvah* when their menstrual period is over. A *mikvah* was, therefore, absolutely essential for the continuation of normal life in the fortress. There were, in fact, two such installations in Masada (a second one was discovered in one of the rooms in the casement wall near the Southern Gate).

Ritual Law lays down the specifications for a *mikvah;* among others, the water must be natural — rain, spring or river water — flowing freely, and not carried to the bath in vessels. Even nowadays, this requirement causes great difficulties in building these baths. The usual method is to construct two pools, or pits. One is filled with rain-water, the other contains ordinary, or tap water. Between the two pools is a connecting hole which is kept closed. When the *mikvah* is to be used for immersion, the stopper is removed and the water in the two pools mixes; the mixture of rain-water with the drawn water "purifies" the latter. The *mikvah* baths at Masada have all the necessary qualifications. An open plastered conduit leads into one pool (the storage pit) and this is connected to another pool (the immersion pit). Beside them was found a smaller, separate pool, which was used for bathing before the ritual immersion. Israeli rabbis, experts in Jewish Law, examined the baths at Masada and pronounced that they met the ritual specifications in every detail.

Another find, indicative of the piety of Masada's defenders, is the synagogue. This is just to the north of the Western Gate through which one enters the plateau from Silva's ramp; the gate itself dates from the Byzan-

77

77. The Byzantine gate on the western side. It seems that the monks' main entrance was from the west.

78

78. Three columns in the synagogue. The steps in the background were the seats for the congregants.

tine period. The synagogue is partly within the casement wall and partly protrudes into the plateau. It seems that the Zealots redesigned the building they found. Originally there had been an entrance chamber to the east and a large room with two rows of columns. The Zealots added walls to create a small chamber to the west, and demolished the wall between the entrance chamber and the main room. On the basis of that wall they placed the two columns that they had removed to make the small chamber.

Around the sides of the large hall they had thus created, they constructed rising rows of seats, amphitheatre-style. The seats were of stone, some of which had been taken from other buildings, notably the Northern Palace, and plastered over. The building has two levels; the lower dates from the reign of Herod, and the upper was added by the Zealots. The Roman garrison apparently used the premises as a stable, as animal droppings were found between the two floors.

When the building was first discovered the archaeologists hesitated to describe it as a synagogue. They were fairly certain that it was, because it faced the right direction — namely, Jerusalem — and the door was in the east, as required. If it was a synagogue, then it was the earliest ever discovered and, furthermore, for at least some part of its history, it was in use while the Temple in Jerusalem was still standing. To claim a find of such significance was only possible on the basis of absolute certainty. Then the archaeologists discovered storage pits between the two floors, containing biblical scrolls, and their doubts vanished. They announced that they had uncovered the synagogue of the Zealots of Masada. Professor Yadin believes that the building had served as a synagogue in Herod's time, too, for use by his family and Jewish members of his entourage. The scrolls found were part of the Book of Ezekiel (the Vision of the Dry Bones), and the last portion of Deuteronomy. Possibly the scrolls were unfit for ritual use, for some reason, and were therefore put away; or, perhaps, they were hidden just before the end so that the Romans would not defile them. A large number of coins was found scattered on the floor of the building, and in the small chamber there were signs of a fire. Perhaps the Zealots set all the furnishings and precious objects ablaze. Understandably, this building is charged with great emotional significance for Jews, and it has become customary to hold *Bar Mitzvah* ceremonies there.

79

79. This picture was taken from inside the synagogue looking out on the plateau. The synagogue is orientated towards Jerusalem.

80

80. The entrance to the small room added to the synagogue during the Zealot occupation of Masada.

Not far from the synagogue, to the east, stands another house of prayer, but of a different faith. This is the church built by the Byzantine monks, the last inhabitants of Masada. This building was in better condition than the rest, being, after all, considerably younger. The walls were still partly upright, and had already attracted the attention of the explorers who visited Masada in the last century, and been identified by them.

The apse in the main hall of the church faces east and the walls were well plastered and decorated with pieces of pottery and small pebbles set into the plaster in geometric designs. According to de Saulcy, the hall had a

81

81. A detail of the wall in the Byzantine church. The bits of pottery set into the plaster form geometrical designs.

82. In this general view of the church wall the overall design is clearly seen.

82

83. The church faced east. The window looks out over the Dead Sea. The beautiful mosaic floor in this room was vandalized.

83

mosaic floor and he writes that he took a few loose pieces with him as a memento of his visit. Others, apparently, followed suit, because except for a small portion at the northern end, the mosaic had disappeared; only two small sections of the western corners were found. The archaeologists now turned their attention to the adjoining chamber and were very pleasantly surprised: they discovered an almost intact mosaic floor, consisting of 16 roundels, some of them enclosing geometric designs and other such motifs as trees, grapes, pomegranates, and a basket of eggs decorated with a crucifix. Not far from the church they discovered the workshop in which the pieces for the church mosaics were cut. The area was covered with thousands of scattered stone cubes.

A little to the north-west of the church, between it and the storehouses, stands a large structure surrounding a central courtyard. Because it is made up of identical units, the archaeologists concluded that it served as the living quarters of the high officials of Herod's court and, later, of the Zealot leaders. Each unit consists of a large room (or courtyard) and two small rooms. Additions were made to the building by the Zealots who needed more living space, and the Byzantine monks erected another structure in the courtyard. This "apartment house" is noteworthy for the coins, particularly shekels, that were discovered in its rooms.

In one room a hoard of silver coins wrapped in cloth had been hidden under the floor. It consisted of 38 shekels and half-shekels in almost mint condition. Near this find, a bronze cash-box was found which contained another 6 shekels and 6 half-shekels. Together with the ones found in the wall chambers, this constitutes the largest find of shekels.

84

84. A detail from the mosaic discovered in the side chamber of the church.
85. The "apartment house". The ruins have retained the symmetry of its construction.
86. This silver shekel from Masada was minted in the fifth year of the revolt. The inscriptions read "Sacred Jerusalem" and "A shekel of Israel".

85

86

87. *A detail of the mysterious Columbarium.*

88. *A general view. The niches in the walls obviously served some function in this building. Unfortunately, no one knows what that function was.*

The work of the archaeologist is very like that of the detective. His discoveries are the clues from which he must reconstruct a past state of affairs. The Masada archaeologists have presented us with a fairly complete picture of life on the mountain, into which all their discoveries fit. However, southeast of the Western Palace they discovered a building which has defied even their considerable ingenuity. This is a circular structure with a wall dividing it. Both the circumference wall and the interior one have small brick-sized niches all over them. The building is known as the Columbarium, meaning "dovecote", because it was originally thought that it may have served to house pigeons, either as carriers for the royal communications system, or for pleasure. The Talmud states that Herod was an enthusiastic pigeon breeder, and that a certain type of dove was named after him. But then one of Professor Yadin's team who was also a pigeon fancier brought a small one to Masada, to see whether it would fit into a niche -- and it did not! The Columbarium theory collapsed. Others have suggested that the building was meant to serve Herod's non-Jewish courtiers (or possibly the Roman garrison) for depositing the ashes of their dead. (Judaism forbids cremation and insists on interment, so if that was the purpose of the structure it could only have served gentiles.) The building had been richly decorated, and various finds show that it was used by both the Zealots and the Byzantine monks. In the north-western section of the casement wall there are two towers with similar niches in their walls.

89

90

89. A detail from one of the Columbarium towers. The niches here present the same problem as those of the Columbarium.

90. The view from one of the Columbarium towers in the western section of the casemate wall.

One of the most vivid illustrations of the luxury of Herod's Masada is the bathhouse which stands north of the storehouse complex, beside Herod's private palace. For size and sophistication, this bathhouse, on a mountain-top in the middle of a wilderness, would not have shamed a fair-sized Roman or Greek town. It consists of a front courtyard and four

91

91. Where did Herod's engineers expect to find the fuel to heat the caldarium in the bathhouse? Perhaps these trees at the foot of Masada provide part of the answer.

rooms: a *caldarium* (hot room); a *tepidarium*, a *frigidarium*, and an entrance-hall which also served as the changing room. The *frigidarium* was a small room which contained a cold-water pool. The pool and the steps leading down into it were plastered, so that the water would not seep through the porous stone. This was the simplest room of the four; one did not spend a long time in the cold water, so no effort was made to delight the bather. The *tepidarium*, the warm room, in which the bather rested before and after the hot room, was beautifully decorated with murals, and had a fine black-and-white tiled floor. Few of the floor tiles were found and it is thought that when the Roman garrison left Masada in A.D. 111,

92. This bath was built in the dressing-room adjoining the bathhouse either by the Zealots or the Romans. They were not concerned about aesthetics and built it against the murals and on the mosaic floor.

92

93

the soldiers took the tiles with them. The *caldarium* is the most interesting part of the bathhouse. This room had a double floor, the top one resting on more than 200 small pillars. A heating unit outside the building pumped hot air into the space between the floors; from here rectangular clay pipes carried the hot air into the room. The pipes were perforated along their sides, so that the heat spread throughout the room. Many of these pipes were found on the site, some still in their original positions in the walls. On one side of the hot room there was a quartz tub standing in a recess. It was filled with water under pressure through a lead pipe from the outside; the water was sprayed over the room and turned into steam.

All these rooms were luxuriously decorated; apparently even their ceilings were painted. The courtyard originally had a row of columns around it, on which rested a roof or a canopy. Only two of the columns, at the entrance to the changing room, were found in their place, but in the bathhouse and in other buildings pedestals of other columns were found, as they had been reused by the Zealots. The bathhouse itself had undergone several modifications. The excavators concluded that the original builders had changed the floor design in the course of the construction and, later, the Zealots added a smaller bath and put benches around the walls. There can be no doubt that this building was one of the social centres of Masada. Anyone who has ever spent a day in the gruelling heat of the Judaean Desert will appreciate what this facility meant to the occupants.

The cost in labour and money that went into building Masada was tremendous, and so, no doubt, was the hardship endured by the builders and workers. The resultant luxury is astounding, when one remembers that these edifices were not erected in a place of human settlement, but on a rock in the desert.

93. The floor of the hot room was built on these small pillars and hot air was pumped into the space thus created.

Perhaps the most striking structure in this impressive place is the palace at the northern end of the summit. This was a private palace, or villa, a less formal residence where the king and his favourites could while away the hours. The technical difficulties involved in building this palace were exceptional even for Masada. Nowhere is Herod's passion for building amazing and dramatic edifices so plainly manifested as in this villa, hanging over the abyss.

94. The view from the northern prow of Masada. On a clear day the oasis at Ein Gedi can be seen.

The northern end of the plateau resembles the prow of a ship, ending in a point. Below it are three giant stairs. These steps are only a few metres wide, but they are very prominent on the profile of the mountain, making it easily recognizable. The ruins on these steps had been noticed when Masada was first identified, and it was assumed that they were fortifications. Josephus gave a detailed description of the palace on Masada and, until the 1950s, the archaeologists assumed that he was referring to the Western Palace, described above.

"He [Herod] built a palace, too, on the western slope, below the fortifications on the crest and inclining in a northerly direction. The palace wall was of great height and strongly built, with 90-foot towers at the four corners. The design of the apartments within, the colonnades and bathrooms, was varied and magnificent, the supporting pillars cut from a single block in every case, the partition walls and floors of the rooms paved with stones of many hues.... A sunken road led from the palace to the hilltop invisible from the outside."

The obvious discrepancies between this description and the Western Palace as uncovered by the archaeologists were ascribed to inaccuracies on the part of Josephus, who had presumably let his imagination run away with him. Applied to that palace, the report is completely wrong: the Western Palace

95. These capitals now decorate Herod's Northern Palace.

96. The three "steps" of the northern palace from the west. The columns on the lowest step were reconstructed from the stone drums found there.

is within the wall, and not "below the fortifications", nor is it "inclining in a northerly direction". Furthermore, no remains were found of a "palace wall of great height", or of a "sunken road". In the early 1950s the first ascent of Masada from the north was made, and the ruins on the northern steps were seen close up. It was immediately realized that these were not the remains of fortifications but of a palace. One of the main objectives of Yadin's dig was to investigate the northern steps, after which Josephus' account was found to be substantially correct.

97

97. The plastered wall which separated the Northern Palace from the rest of the summit and gave Herod the privacy he desired.

The Northern Palace was separated from the rest of the plateau by an enormous plastered wall which rose across the northern edge. Beyond this wall the summit narrows to form the first step. A gate near the eastern end of the wall was the only entrance into the palace. The upper level of the palace is slightly higher than that of the storehouses, the bathhouse and administrative building, which are closest to it. This level contained Herod's living quarters, which consisted of four rooms and a semicircular balcony looking towards Ein Gedi. The rooms were lavishly decorated, and the floors were paved with black and white mosaics in geometric patterns. The middle level was a balcony built on a peculiar circular structure, the remains of which look like a cone within a cone. It seems that this was the solution to

98

98. *The remains of the structure on the middle level. It appears that its function was to support the floor of this level of the palace.*

99. *False columns at the back of the middle level. These were built against the wall to give an impression of depth.*

99

the engineering problem of constructing a flat area without an adequate base. This level probably had a roof supported by columns. The lowest level, today the most impressive, contained a large hall and a patio. The hall was magnificently decorated and large sections of its murals were preserved under the rubble that had covered them for many centuries. The back

100

100. *A close-up of the structural basis of the middle level.*
101. *One of the column capitals discovered on the lowest "step". The intricate carving is a good illustration of the aesthetic standards of the builders.*
102. *The columns on the lowest level as they appear today.*

101

102

(southern) wall had half-pillars moulded out of the plaster to create an illusion of depth. One of the major problems faced by the Yadin expedition was how to preserve the wall paintings so that they could be left *in situ*, and withstand the weather and the visitors. Experts were brought from all over the world and many different systems were tried, including removing the whole layer of plaster from the wall and strengthening it with special adhesive. The paintings are there today, where they were originally executed, and it is hoped that they will remain in good condition for future generations to admire.

103. The frescoes on the lower level of Herod's Northern Palace. The Yadin expedition invested enormous efforts in the restoration of these unique paintings, particularly in order to leave them in situ *so that visitors to Masada would be able to see this part of the palace as it was in Herod's time.*

103

The middle level is some 20 metres below the upper, and the bottom level is 15 metres below that. A staircase connected the three levels, but unfortunately only parts have survived. Today the two lower levels of the palace are reached by a staircase hanging on the side of the mountain. A considerable engineering feat in itself, it was executed by engineering units of the Israel Defence Forces.

104. The foot of the staircase leading up from the lowest level of the palace. Unfortunately, over the centuries most of the staircase was destroyed.

104

105. A view of the mountainside between the top and the middle levels.
106. The staircase hanging on the side of the mountain as seen from the lowest level. The fence along the top protects people who stand on the summit. The support-walls of the middle level can be clearly seen.

105

107

107. This was the view King Herod saw when he looked to the north. It has not changed since his time. The haze over the Dead Sea is the result of the intense evaporation of this desert lake.

Why did Herod invest such enormous efforts into building this amazing villa? Several reasons have been proposed. First, that it afforded him absolute privacy; in the villa he was completely cut off from the activities on the summit. Second, that it gave him an incomparable view to the east, north and west. The third, and perhaps the most important, is that the villa is in the shade for most of the day and, on a bare mountain-top in the desert, near the Dead Sea, where the sun beats down unmercifully for most months of the year, this is a very important consideration. In addition, nestling against the northern flank of the mountain gave the villa perfect protection from the vicious south wind which so often blows on Masada.

108

110

109

108. A sandal discovered in the bathhouse of the northern palace. It was found beside a skeleton of a young woman.
109. This plait of hair was perhaps the most moving discovery of the archaeologists.
110. The staircase into the bathhouse of Herod's villa.

On the lowest floor of the villa, Herod had installed a small bathhouse with all the conveniences, albeit in miniature, of the large bathhouse on the summit. Here, too, there was a hot room and a heating facility. When the excavators turned their attention to this part of the villa, they received an unpleasant shock. Amongst evidence of a great fire they discovered the skeletons of a young man, a young woman and a child. Beside the young man's bones they found weapons, silver-plated armour scales and parts of a prayer shawl; near the young woman lay her plaited hair, perfectly preserved in the dry atmosphere, wrapped in a kerchief, and her sandals. Can these be the remains of one of the Zealot commanders and his family? Is this the visible, physical proof of the truth of Josephus' story? —

"So finally the nine [men remaining after the mass suicide] *presented their throats, and the one man left till last first surveyed the serried ranks of the dead, in case, amidst all the slaughter someone was still left in need of his hand; then finding that all had been dispatched set the place blazing fiercely, and summoning all his strength drove his sword right through his body and fell dead by the side of his family."*

On that 15th day of the month of Nisan (2 May, A.D. 73; though some scholars believe it was in 74), after the earthwork wall had burned down, it was plain even to the Zealots that Masada would fall. The Romans returned to their camps and intensified the watch on the siege wall to make sure that no one escaped. They prepared for the final assault. But, as Josephus puts it, Eleazar, the commander of Masada, had no intention of trying to escape, or of allowing anyone else to do so. He knew only too well what would be the fate of the survivors and he decided that the only honourable way out was death.

"Making up his mind that in the circumstances this [death] was the wisest course, he collected the toughest of his comrades and urged it upon them in a speech of which this was the substance:

'My loyal followers, long ago we resolved to serve neither the Romans nor anyone else but only God, who alone is the true and righteous Lord of men: now the time has come that bids us prove our determination by our deeds . . . we have never submitted to slavery, even when it brought no danger with it; we must not choose slavery now, and with its penalties that will mean the end of everything if we fall alive into the hands of the Romans . . . . And I think that it is God who has given us this privilege, that we can die nobly and as free men . . .'"

111. The physical evidence of the inexorable Roman siege of Masada. The camps and the siege-wall made escape impossible.

112. This detail from Titus' triumphal arch in Rome illustrates the fate Masada's defenders were determined to avoid — being brought to Rome as captive slaves, like their predecessors shown here carrying the Menorah *(candelabrum) from the destroyed Temple.*

Obviously, it was Josephus who composed the speeches that he put in Eleazar's mouth, and some scholars discern in them the influence of Stoic philosophy — which Eleazar would have rejected. On the other hand, as a former commander in the revolt against Rome, Josephus must have been familiar with the ideology of the Zealots. But whether or not Josephus' version of Eleazar's speech has a basis in fact, it is the only one we possess.

Eleazar goes on to proclaim that their defeat must be the punishment for the sins of the Jews, else "He would not have shut his eyes to the destruction of so many thousands, or allowed His most holy city to be burnt to the ground".

"For these wrongs lets us pay the penalty not to our bitterest enemies, the Romans, but to God — by our own hands. It will be easier to bear. Let our wives die unabused, our children without knowledge of slavery; after that, let us do each other an ungrudging kindness, preserving our freedom as a glorious winding sheet."

Eleazar suggested that they burn their possessions and the whole fortress, so that there would be nothing left for the Romans. Only the food supplies should be spared, to bear witness that the men of Masada did not die of want.

The speech did not meet with unanimous, enthusiastic approval, and Eleazar proceeded to make an even more impassioned plea in which he extolled death. "Death gives freedom to our souls", and there is no need to fear it more than sleep which we all enjoy. He reviewed the revolt against Rome, stating again that it was God's will and they should not oppose it:

113. These storehouses were burned by the Zealots, determined to leave nothing for the Roman enemy.

113

"After all, we were born to die, we and those we brought into the world: this even the luckiest must face". He described the alternative: their women would be ravished and their children taken captive before their very eyes, and they would be powerless to prevent it.

One cannot help feeling that Josephus was using Eleazar as a spokesman to express ideas which he, perhaps, partly wished he had been brave — or proud — enough to carry out. For, without doubt, these speeches are charged with intense emotion. This time Eleazar's oratory had the desired effect and, to a man, Masada's defenders decided to burn down the fortress, kill their wives and children and do away with themselves.

We have seen conclusive evidence that the Zealots of Masada were pious Jews; their decision to commit suicide, therefore, raises serious problems. The Jewish religion, then as now, condemns suicide in no uncertain terms. Life is God's gift, and no one has the right to terminate his own or another's. How then could these devout Jews do what they did? Were it not that archaeology has substantiated so many of Josephus' descriptions, it would be easy to dismiss the story as a figment of Josephus' literary imagination, as a fine dramatic ending to a tale of heroism. But the excavations at Masada have shown Josephus to be a reliable, painstaking historian. To make up the speeches for the protagonists of his history — that was common practice until fairly recent times. To make up major events, such as this one, which must have been talked about by the Roman legionnaires, would be excessive. But a question remains, and all answers are unsatisfactory.

114. The bones found in the southern cave were re-interred in this grave which was dug for them on the assault ramp.

114

It has been suggested that the Zealots saw surrender as tantamount to idolatry, and Jews are supposed to sacrifice their lives rather than worship idols. This is true, but the Law says that the Jew must let himself be killed rather than commit that sin — not that he should kill himself! Another difficulty is that Josephus is the only source for the Masada story, and it is very strange that there is no mention or even hint of it in the Talmud, that enormous compendium of Jewish Law and lore. Rabbinic literature of this period and the one following makes no mention of Masada. Other chapters of the revolt against Rome, such as the destruction of Jerusalem, or the meeting between Rabbi Johanan ben Zakkai and Vespasian, are discussed in detail. Why not Masada? Can it be that they disapproved so strongly of the final step?

The mass suicide of 960 persons was not an easy decision to carry out. The way it was done was that each man killed his own wife and children, and then lots were drawn and ten men were chosen to kill the rest. Then one of the ten was chosen, also by lot, to kill the others, and finally himself. Of the many important finds on Masada, Professor Yadin describes as the most moving the discovery of 11 small ostraca in the north-western section of the plateau, near the entrance to the Northern Palace. On each of these shards of pottery was written a single name and nothing more; all seem to have been written by the same hand. They may have been nicknames adopted by the fighters, or given them by their comrades. One of the names was Joav, an uncommon name in those days; it means "daring", and was presumably given because of the person's bravery. One of the pieces bore the name Ben Yaïr, and on Masada this can only refer to the commander, Eleazar ben Yaïr. Were these the lots cast to choose the last ten men and then the last one?

115. Some of the ostraca found near the storehouses. It is conjectured that they were the lots used to choose the ten men who killed the others and the last survivor who had to finish the gruesome task.

116

116. The two women and five children who survived probably hid in one of the conduits or staircases, such as the one pictured here.

The defenders thought that no one would live to tell the tale. They were wrong. Two women, one of them a relative of Eleazar, and five children, hid in one of the water conduits. When, on the morrow, the Romans entered the fortress, expecting a bitter struggle and finding only smouldering desolation, they emerged from their hiding place and told what had happened.

"Seeing no enemy, but dreadful solitude on every side, fire within, and silence, they [the Romans] were at a loss to guess what had happened. At last, as if giving the signal for a volley, they shouted, in the hope that some of those inside would show themselves. The noise came to the ears of the women, who emerged from the conduits and gave the Romans a detail-

117

117. The medal struck to commemorate Masada.

118. The Israeli flag on the summit symbolizes the pride and tragedy of Masada.

ed account of what had happened, the second of them providing a lucid report of Eleazar's speech and the action that had followed. They found it difficult to believe her. . . . When they came upon the rows of dead bodies, they did not exult over them as enemies but admired the nobility of their resolve, and the way in which so many had shown in carrying it out without a tremor an utter contempt of death."

Flavius Silva left a garrison at Masada which probably remained there till A.D. 111, the date of the latest coin found. Scholars believe that the Romans remained at Masada at least 40 years.

Although Josephus' account of Masada was known for centuries, it took on a special significance with the beginning of the Jewish return to the Holy Land at the turn of the last century, and the early decades of this. Today the State of Israel considers itself to be the legitimate successor of the kingdom of Judaea, whose last stand was at Masada. The place and its history have a profound moral and emotional significance to Israelis. The excavations and restoration conducted by Professor Yadin were followed with intense interest by the general public, and press conferences were breathlessly awaited to hear what new and thrilling finds would be revealed. The Government had a Masada medal struck and a set of Masada postage stamps issued to commemorate the discovery.

Restored Masada is a major attraction for Israelis as well as visitors from overseas. Individually and in groups they come to the mountain to see the theatre of one of history's greatest dramas. Certain Israeli army units hold the final parades of their basic training courses on the summit of Masada. On these occasions the slogan "Masada will not fall again!" is borne in fiery letters against the night sky.

But Masada is more than a national symbol for Israelis. Rome wanted to rule the world and succeeded for some time. She imposed her own order, the *Pax Romana*, and swallowed up countless small nations. The Empire, even when ruled by the relatively democratic Senate, dominated all within its orbit by sheer force of arms. Only the mighty eastern nations, by virtue of their size and distance from Rome, withstood her greed and ambition. The smaller, nearer nations fell one after the other. The 960 individuals

119

on Masada refused to succumb, preferring death to surrender. The story of Masada has captured the imagination, and the site in which it unfolded, with its blend of luxury and horror, has made it more vivid.

Its message is the message of freedom fighting against tyranny, of the might of the spirit against the might of empires. The message is still alive.

119. A Bar Mitzvah *ceremony celebrated in the Masada synagogue.*

ADDITIONAL PHOTOGRAPHY

Alinari (Nos. 11, 112); Bank of Israel (No. 86); Bibliothèque Nationale, Paris (No. 25); Shlomo S. Gafni (Nos. 31, 32, 37, 41, 60, 64, 70, 74, 75, 95, 104, 110, 111, 114); Photo Garo (No. 13); Government Press Office (No. 119); David Harris (No. 46); Israel Coins and Medals Corporation Ltd. (No. 117); Israel Exploration Society (Nos. 17, 109, 115); Israel Museum, the Shrine of the Book (No. 44); Zev Radovan (Nos. 39, 40, 108).